The Nels[illegible]
fro[illegible]
Grama & Granpa Naut
May 1984
Logan, Utah

Because we love you!

THE FORCE INSIDE YOU

BY SLIM GOODBODY

PHOTOGRAPHS BY BRUCE CURTIS

ILLUSTRATIONS BY NURIT KARLIN

COWARD-McCANN, INC. NEW YORK

Initial Research by Mary Ellen Rohon

Published simultaneously in Canada by General Publishing Co. Limited, Toronto.
First printing
Printed in the United States of America
Costume constructed at Ray Diffen Stage Clothes, Inc., New York
Design by Mike Suh

Library of Congress Cataloging in Publication Data
Burstein, John.
The force inside you.
Includes index.
Summary: Presents a series of exercises for mind and body gathered from all over the world, ranging from Cherokee lore to the wisdom of ancient Greeks, which can help develop human abilities and enable one to become a more powerful person.
1. Senses and sensations—Problems, exercises, etc.—Juvenile literature. 2. Mind and body—Problems, exercises, etc.—Juvenile literature. 3. Exercises for children—Juvenile literature. [1. Exercise]
I. Karlin, Nurit, ill. II. Curtis, Bruce, ill.
III. Title.
BF233.B88 1983 158'.1 83-2034
ISBN 0-698-20589-8
ISBN 0-698-20593-6 (pbk.)

CONTENTS

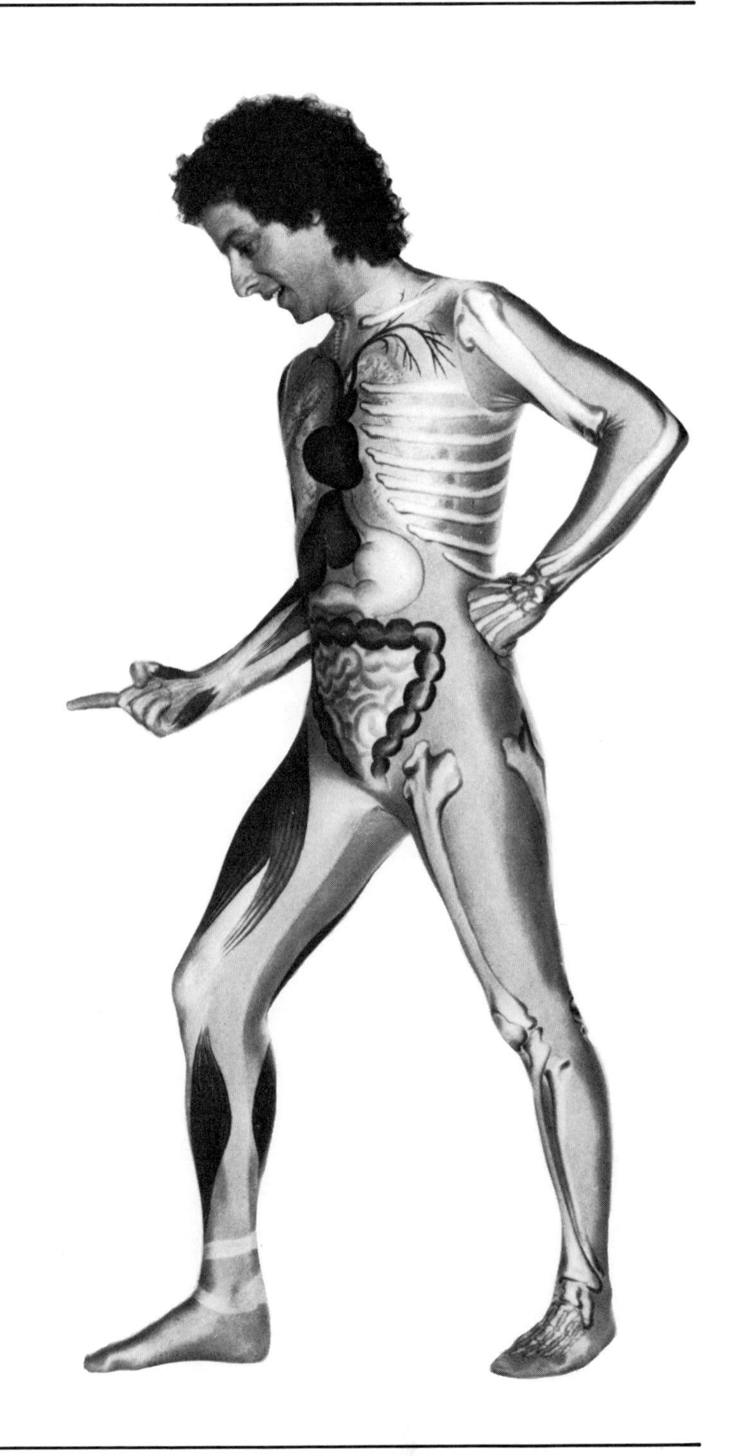

INTRODUCTION

My book is all about The Force.

The Force Inside You!

Not X-ray vision, super-strength, lightning speed, or Jedi power, for these are all make-believe. What I'll be showing you are some very special (and sometimes secret) ways to develop your own human abilities.

These are skills you can't learn in school, but all of them can teach you to become a more powerful person.

It's taken me a long time to gather all of this information together for you. I've had to collect it from all kinds of sources:

- I've discovered the exercises the ancient Greeks used to develop balance, and
- what Roman citizens did to heal themselves.
- From an African tribe I learned body awareness and flexibility,
- and a Cherokee chief taught me the Secret of Still Moving.
- Olympic athletes showed me how to relax,
- and a yogi from India demonstrated a better way of breathing.
- Some of the exercises I've developed myself.
- Some came to me in dreams,
- and I've promised never to reveal who taught me others.

These exercises will help you discover, uncover, and develop the Force Inside You.

GROWING UP

When you were born, you got some terrific birthday presents:

- A human body—all wrapped up in skin with thousands of working parts within;
- A human mind—able to think, dream, feel, imagine, and serve as your body's control center;
- A world to live in—filled with people to know, places to go, and things to do;
- A whole lifetime—to spend exploring and learning to use all you've been given.

Just as there are seasons in a year, there are also seasons in a person's life. Right now you're in the springtime of your years. During this season of rapid growth, you have a great opportunity to develop your powers. Your body is strong, your mind is quick, and your spirit is full of life.

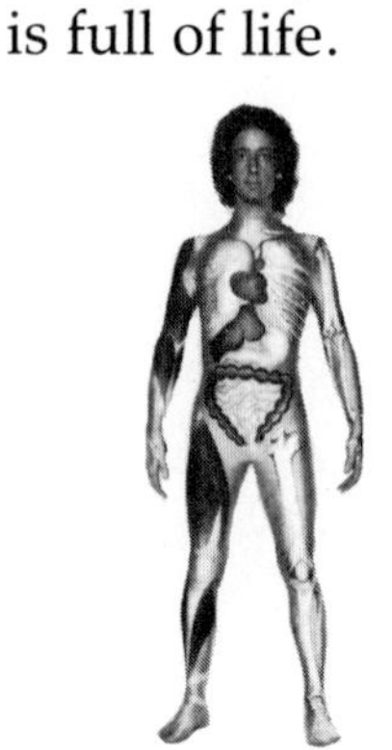

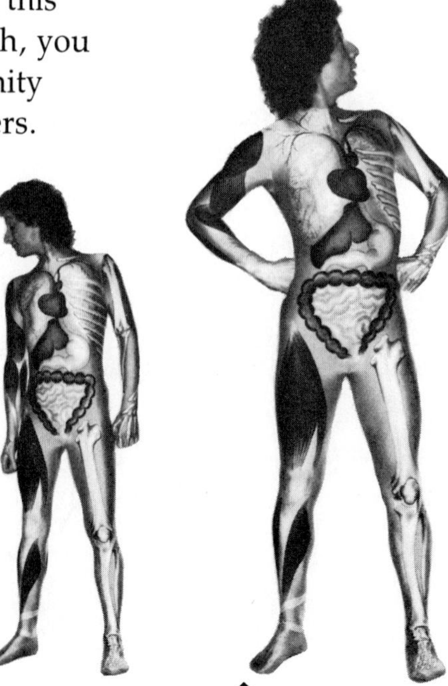

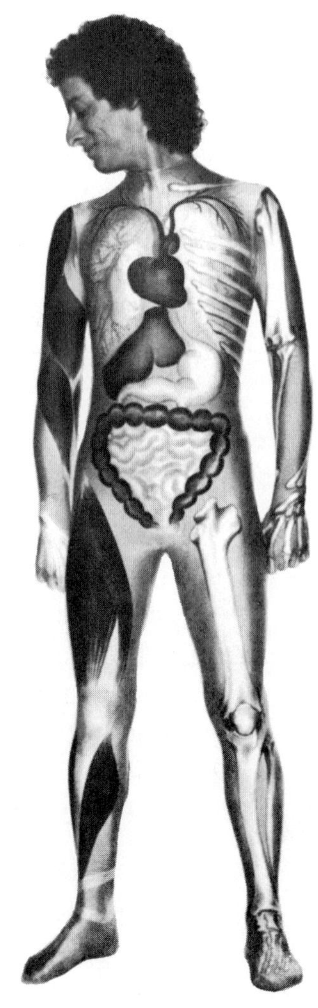

Growing up is a very special time.

I like to think that there are two kinds of growth:

1. The kind that happens to you and
2. The kind that you make happen.

The first kind of growing pretty much takes care of itself. Without having to think about it, certain things happen. Your body gets bigger, your hair grows longer, teeth grow in, you learn to walk and talk, and your feelings for others develop.

The second kind of growing happens only if you work at it. It takes practice, patience, and determination to do things like ride a bike, learn to be a good friend, catch a ball, swim in a lake, or bake a cake. But a lot of the fun we get out of living comes from this kind of growth.

If you stop to think about it, there is really no limit to the things you can learn to do. Being a human being is an Adventure in Growing.

And, every day, you have the chance to develop the Force Inside You!

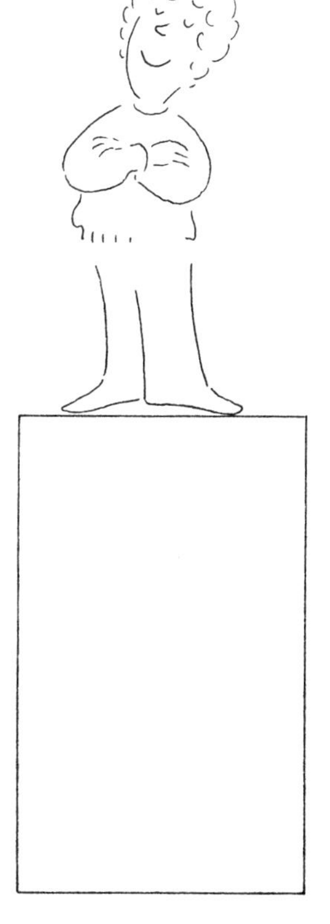

THE BODY'S FORCE

Most people live in their heads. It's not that they don't have bodies, it's just that they don't pay much attention to them. During the day, bodies are covered up with clothes, and at night they're tucked away under the covers. In school, they're plopped behind desks, and at home they're plopped in front of the television set. The truth is, except for a few athletes and performers, most people forget about their bodies most of the time.

To prove my point, let me ask you these questions:

> What is your body doing right now?
> If you're sitting, what position are your legs in? Stretched out in front of you? Bent? Crossed?
> Are both feet touching the ground? In the same way?
> Is your back straight or hunched over?
> Which part of your body is touching the chair?
> How far are your elbows from your sides?
> Is one shoulder lifted a little higher than the other?

I'm sure you can answer these questions, but I bet it took you a moment or two to check things out. You probably weren't aware of your own body until I asked you what it was doing.

The exercises in this chapter will help you learn more about how your body works and how you can work with your body.

BODY AWARENESS

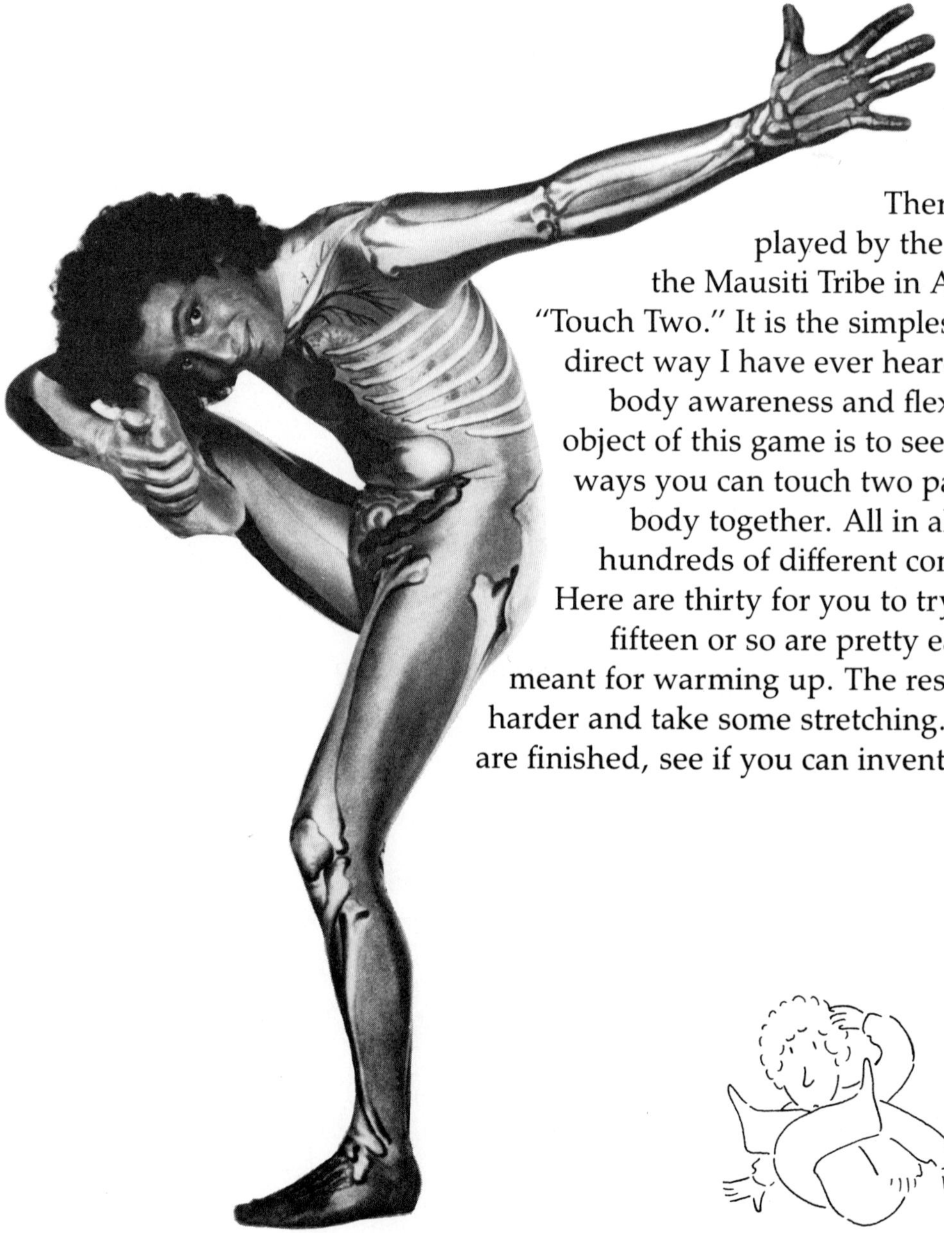

There is a game played by the children of the Mausiti Tribe in Africa called "Touch Two." It is the simplest and most direct way I have ever heard of to gain body awareness and flexibility. The object of this game is to see how many ways you can touch two parts of your body together. All in all, there are hundreds of different combinations. Here are thirty for you to try.* The first fifteen or so are pretty easy and are meant for warming up. The rest are a little harder and take some stretching. When you are finished, see if you can invent fifty more.

1. fingertip to fingertip
2. thumb to thumb
3. palm to palm
4. back of hand to back of hand
5. wrist to wrist
6. elbow to elbow
7. knee to knee
8. ankle to ankle
9. toe to toe
10. sole to sole
11. wrist to wrist (behind your back)
12. elbow to back of knee
13. wrist to shoulder
14. chin to shoulder
15. ear to shoulder
16. heel to knee
17. neck to toe
18. tongue to thumb
19. nose to heel
20. chin to toe
21. heel to chin
22. palms to elbows
23. fingertip to nose with eyes closed
24. fingertip to fingertip behind your neck (in one try)
25. back of hand to back of neck
26. toe to forehead
27. foot to shoulder
28. elbow to toe (while standing)
29. chin to thigh
30. heel to elbow (behind your back)

*You can practice this exercise with a friend, who calls out very quickly the parts to be touched. Time yourself to see how fast you can make it through the list.

WHICH FINGERS ARE WHICH

Here's an experiment to try which proves that people sometimes don't know which fingers are which on their own hand!

Here's what to do:

Ask a friend (or parent) to clasp his or her hands like so.

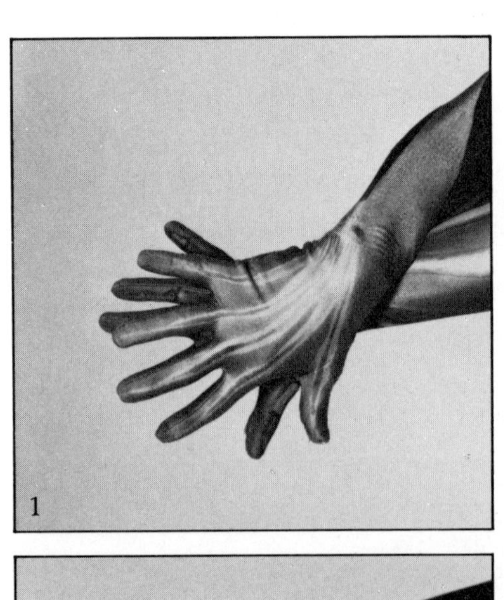

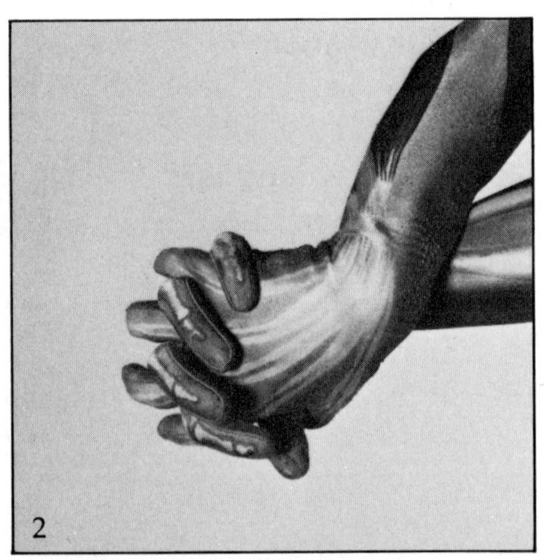

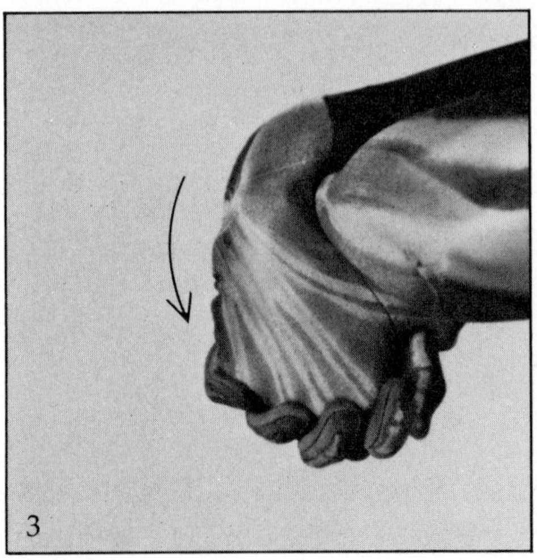

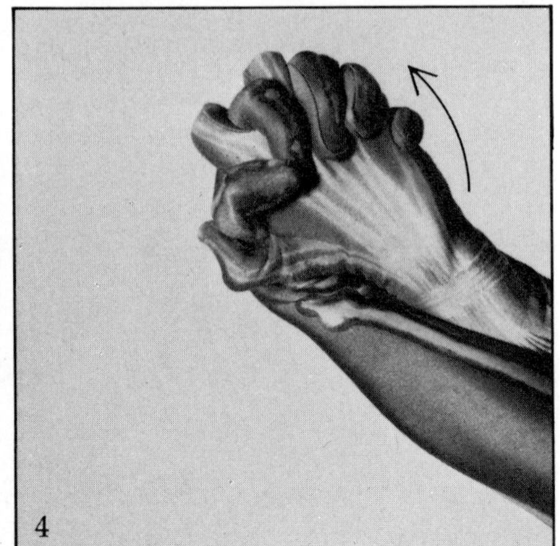

Now, making sure you never actually touch any of the fingers, point to them, one at a time,

and ask your partner to lift them up. Make sure you don't pick the fingers to be raised in any logical order.

You will be amazed at how often your partner lifts the wrong finger.

Now switch around. It's your turn to try

If you practice this exercise for a while, you'll be able to learn WHICH FINGERS ARE WHICH!

HELPING HANDS

Hands are the greatest tools in the world. Just think about all the different things they help you do every day—

- from holding a toothbrush to digging a ditch;
- from catching a football to scratching an itch.

Each of these skills and activities requires strength and flexibility. Here are some exercises you can do to help your helping hands.

1. For strength—

Using a small rubber ball that fits easily into the palm of your hand, practice gripping tightly for a few moments and then relaxing. Make sure that each time you squeeze, you are doing it with all your might and that when you relax, you're relaxing completely. For the best results, do this exercise five times in the morning and five times at night, using both hands. Within a week, your hands will be a lot stronger.

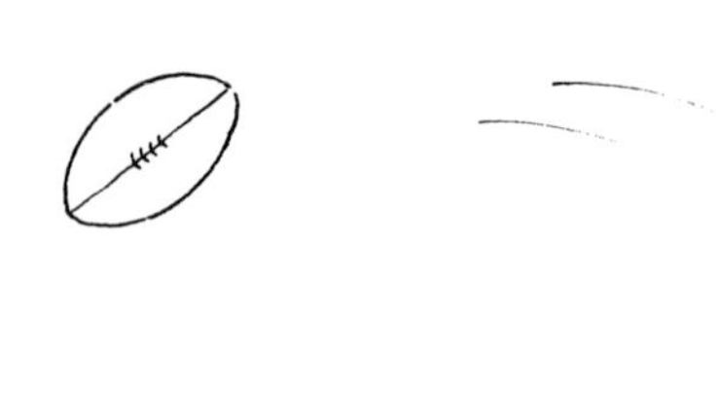

2. For stretch—

Working with a ruler, see how far you can stretch your fingers apart. Measure the distances from:

thumb to pinkie
index finger to pinkie
middle finger to pinkie
ring finger to pinkie
ring to middle
ring to thumb
middle to thumb
index to thumb
index to ring
index to middle

Practice stretching every day and write the numbers down on a stretch chart (like the one you see in the illustration) and see how much farther you can spread your fingers by the end of one week. Remember to practice with both the left and right hand.

3. For flexibility—

Try to hold as many different objects as you can at the same time—like a pencil, a cup, some keys, a napkin, a photograph, a belt, a shirt, etc. Look around you right now and see if there are ten or fifteen small or light objects you can hold at the same time in one hand. See if you can do the same thing with your other hand. (Make sure there's nothing breakable or else do this over something soft.)

TOE RIFFIC FEET

In our last exercise we worked with your hands. Now let's move on down to your feet. We spend so much of our day with our feet tucked inside our shoes that we sometimes forget how incredibly flexible they really are.

In the Orient, where the martial arts of judo, karate and kung-fu began, certain exercises were invented to develop foot power.

Here are two:

1. Warmups:

Stretch your toes out as far and as wide as possible. Hold for a moment, then relax. Do this two times with each foot.

Clench your toes tightly. Hold for a moment, then relax. Do this two times with each foot.

Roll your feet around in circles, really loosening up your ankles. First three times clockwise, then three times counterclockwise.

2. Pickups:

Practice picking up these different objects with your toes. Do it smoothly and quickly.

A pencil
A towel
A book
A crayon
A marble

3. Pull-on:

Take out a sock. See if you can put it on and pull it up using your feet alone. After you do this, take the sock off and put it on the other foot.

4. Toe-Hold:

Put a piece of paper on the floor. Hold a pencil between the first two toes of one foot and try to write your name. Practice until you can do it legibly.

Once you have mastered these exercises, you'll find your feet will work better in all kinds of ways, for instance dancing or kicking a football.

RIGHT LEFT • LEFT RIGHT

Are you a lefty . . . or a righty?

Whichever one you happen to be, you depend upon the muscles on one side of your body more than those on the other side. Even though this is quite natural, you often don't develop as much strength and ability on the unused side as you might.

Have you even heard the word ambidextrous? It means being able to use both hands with equal skill. Some baseball players spend years developing this ability. Here are some exercises you can do to develop yours.

1. The Switcheroo

If you are right-handed, do everything left-handed for a day. Things like:

opening the door
brushing your teeth
writing your name
combing your hair
holding a fork

Of course, if you are left-handed, do everything with your right hand.

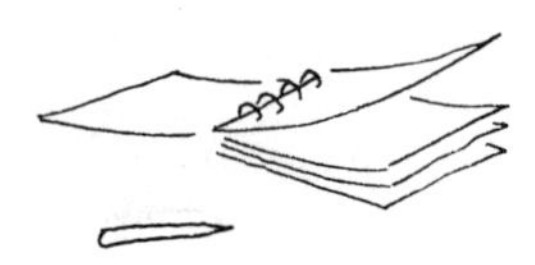

2. One a week

After the first day, pick one thing you want to practice and do it all week long. For instance, turning the doorknob.

Working both left and right is not only good for your body, it's good for your brain. You see, the left side of your brain controls the right side of your body and the right side of your brain controls the left side of your body. When you do the following exercise everything will be working together.

3. The Human Corkscrew

Lie on the floor—legs straight, knees and ankles together. Now twist your head to the right and your legs to the left. Now head to the left and legs to the right. Do this over and over again for a minute or two—very smoothly and without stopping in any one position.

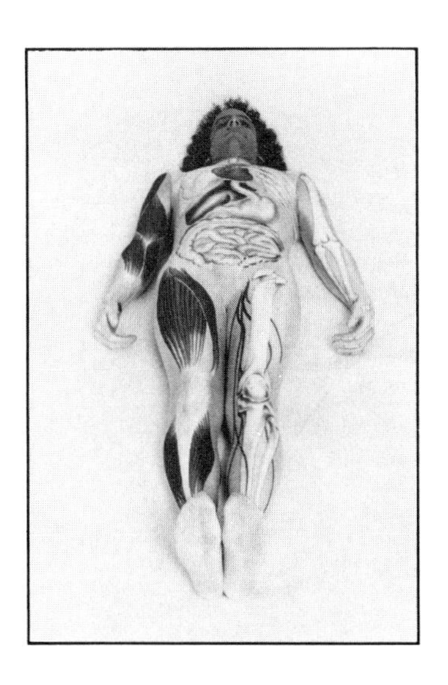

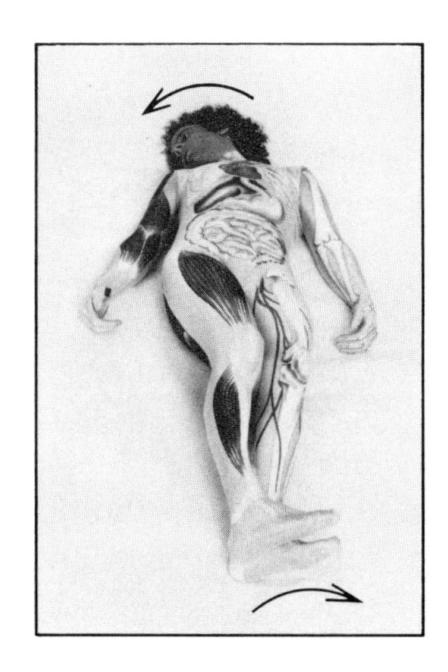

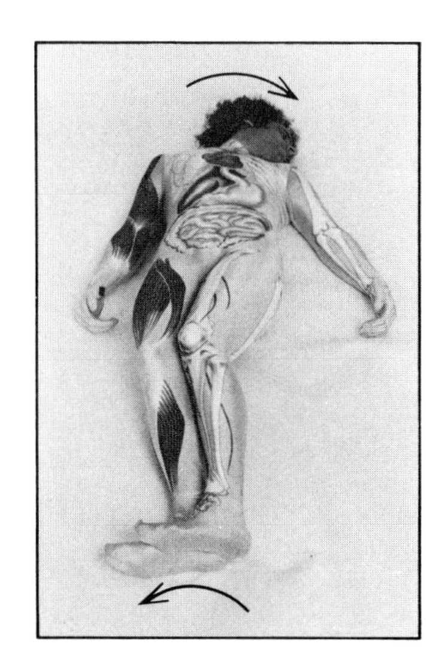

STILL MOVING

There are lots of stories about the ability of Native Americans to move silently through the forest. I was interested in learning how this was done, so I made a trip to Tennessee to visit a very old Cherokee chief who could teach me about it. At first he refused, saying, "These are the old ways, my son. They are not for you modern people." But when I told him that the knowledge he taught me would be used for good, to help people develop their Inner Force, he finally agreed. Here is what he taught me. It's called the Secret of Still Moving and it is made up of several steps that will take a week or two to really learn well.

Step 1: Footwork

A. Practice these four kinds of walking:

a) on tiptoes

b) on your heels

c) on the outside edges of your feet

d) on the inner edges of your feet

Do each of the above for only two or three minutes a day. Soon you'll feel comfortable in all of these positions.

B. Practice walking slowly, rolling your foot down as you go (see illustration). First your heel touches, then your instep, and finally your toes. Walk around the room like this for a few minutes until you're moving along smoothly and evenly. Now change the direction of the roll. First the toe touches, next the instep, and finally the heel. Walk around this way for a few minutes.

Practice both rolls until you feel comfortable doing both.

Step 2: Mental Preparation

Imagine:

a) Your body is filled with air and you are as light as a balloon. Float around the room.

b) You are a feather being blown around the room by the wind.

Step 3: Observe Others

Watch how different animals move—cats, frogs, snakes, insects, and so on. Then try to imitate each one. In this way you'll begin to understand the incredible range of movement possibilities available. As you practice, you'll steadily increase your ability to slip silently from place to place.

Step 4: Putting It All Together

When you have mastered all of these steps, it is time to go out and practice putting all of it together. By now your feet are well trained and can shift instantly if something underfoot is about to make a noise. Your body understands the feeling of moving lightly, your mind can help you become an invisible part of your surroundings and you are able to adopt the movements of different kinds of creatures.

The final step is believing in yourself. You now have the skills, so trust that everything will work together. It will. Still Moving will come naturally and easily.

YOGA BREATH

You take more than 20,000 breaths a day. The oxygen in the air you breathe helps your body change the food you eat into the energy you need. But did you know that most people do not really breathe correctly? Instead of bringing the air deep inside their lungs, they take breaths that are far too shallow.

Here is an exercise that was developed in India thousands of years ago to help people learn how to breathe properly. It has been passed down through the ages by teachers of yoga, and now I pass it along to you.

1. Lie on your back with your knees bent and your feet flat on the floor, shoulder-width apart. Place one hand on your lower abdomen, just below your belly button, and the other hand on your chest. Breathing in and out through your nose, let out all the stale air and then begin inhaling slowly.

2. Feel your abdomen rising up under your hand. This is bringing air deep into your lungs. Actually feel your hand being forced up.

3. Next, let the air move up into your chest. You should feel it sort of "roll up" like a wave. Fill up your body with as much air as you comfortably can.

4. Exhale, and push ALL the air out. This is a very important step, because before you can breathe in fully you must get rid of all the old air.

5. Repeat this thirty times. If you do it every day, you'll be able to change your old habits. You'll soon be taking deeper breaths and feeling more and more energetic.

During the week that you're working on this power breathing exercise, every once in a while check to see how your breathing is going. Not while you're actually practicing, of course, but sometime during the day. This awareness will help you a great deal.

LETTING GO

If you want to develop your strength and power, you've got to be able to relax. Every day you build up tension in your muscles without realizing it. It won't go away unless you spend time letting it go. Once it's gone, energy can flow in and give you a new feeling of zest!

Athletes who train for the Olympics understand this. They know that when their muscles are tense and tight, they can't perform as well. Relaxation frees the muscles, clears the mind, and helps make winners.

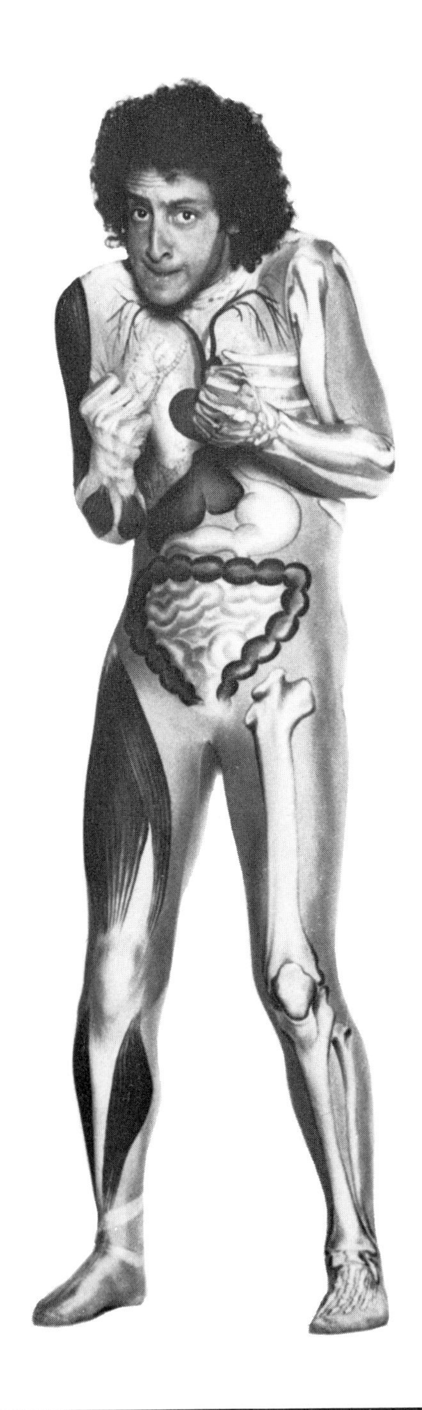
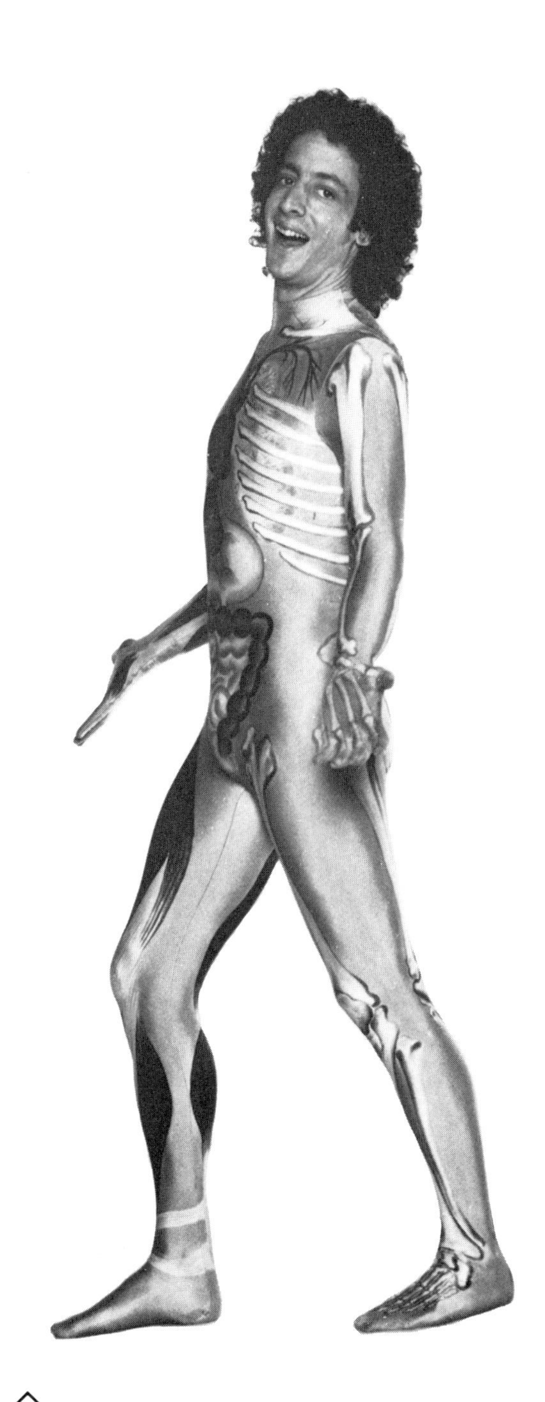

The following Letting-Go exercises are practiced by some members of the United States Olympic Team.

Letting Go #1

Lie down comfortably on your bed or carpeted floor (don't use a pillow), arms at your sides, and close your eyes. Take two or three deep breaths, then—

Press your head back HARD against the bed. Really feel the strain. Hold like this for five seconds . . . then let go and relax for about half a minute.

Scrunch up your face as tightly as possible. Really tense those face muscles . . . hold it for five seconds . . . let go and relax.

Hunch your shoulders . . . hold it . . . let go . . . relax.

Make a fist and tighten your whole left arm . . . hold it . . . let go and relax.

Make a fist and tighten your whole right arm . . . hold it . . . let go . . . relax.

Tighten your buttocks and force your lower back down . . . hold it . . . let go . . . relax.

Tighten your left leg muscles . . . hold it . . . let go . . . relax.

Tighten your right leg muscles . . . hold it . . . let go . . . relax.

Squeeze the toes of your left foot together . . . hold it . . . let go . . . relax.

Squeeze the toes of your right foot together . . . hold it . . . let go . . . relax.

Tighten your whole body . . . hold it . . . let go . . . relax.

When you're finished, stretch and get up slowly. Make sure that during this whole relaxation exercise you keep breathing as deeply and as smoothly as possible. The only time you hold your breath is while you're tensing the muscles for five seconds.

Letting Go #2

Lie on your back, arms at your sides, with your palms up and your feet slightly apart. Take a deep breath in, let it out, and relax. Imagine you can feel the weight of your body sinking into the bed or floor (whichever you are lying on). Feel your body becoming soft, loose, and warm. Every time you exhale, feel your body sinking deeper. Every time you inhale say the word RELAX to yourself.

Do this exercise for five minutes. Open your eyes. Take a big stretch and get up. You'll be feeling very refreshed!

ROMAN HEALTH

When Roman citizens became ill and had to stay in bed, they didn't just lie around waiting to get better. There were certain bed-exercises they practiced to stay in shape and help their bodies heal faster. Next time you're sick, you can try some of them.

1. While lying on your back, stretch your arms high overhead and slowly lower them to your sides. Raise them again and lower them away from your body out toward the sides of the bed (see illustration). Do both several times and rest.

2. Still lying on your back, bring your knees up to your chest and clasp your arms around them. Hold for a minute, let go and lower your legs. Repeat five times.

3. Sit up on the edge of your bed and dangle your feet over the side. Rotate your feet around in circles, first to the left and then to the right. Circle ten times each way.

4. Lie back down, this time without a pillow. Roll your head slowly from left to right and back again several times, until you feel a nice smooth flowing movement. Stop and rest.

5. Wiggle your fingers for one minute.

6. Wiggle your toes for one minute.

7. Take ten deep breaths (through your nose if it's not stuffed up, otherwise through your mouth). Every time you inhale, make sure your chest expands as much as possible. When you exhale, try to squeeze all the air out.

Of course, you may be too sick to try one or more of these exercises, but as you feel better, do what you can. You'll be surprised at how much they can help your health.

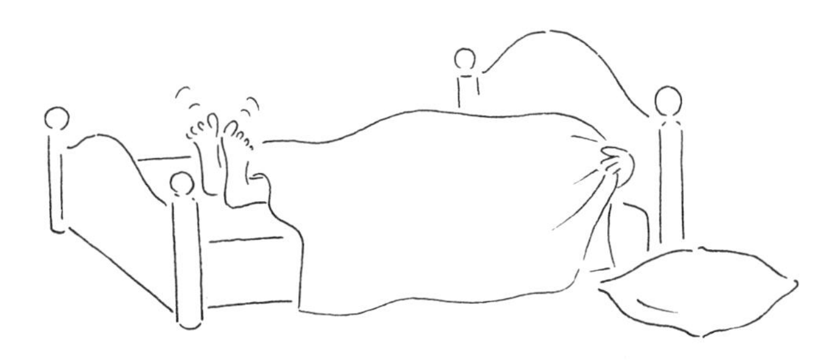

SENSATIONAL FORCE

Simply said, your senses are sensational. Their job is to report information to your brain. The five main senses (sight, hearing, smell, taste, and touch) relay information about the outer world, while your inner senses (hunger, thirst, balance, time, etc.) report on the world within.

Your senses work so well that you probably take them for granted. But there are lots of things you can do to increase their power. Read on . . . and remember: you can always improve yourself. That's common sense.

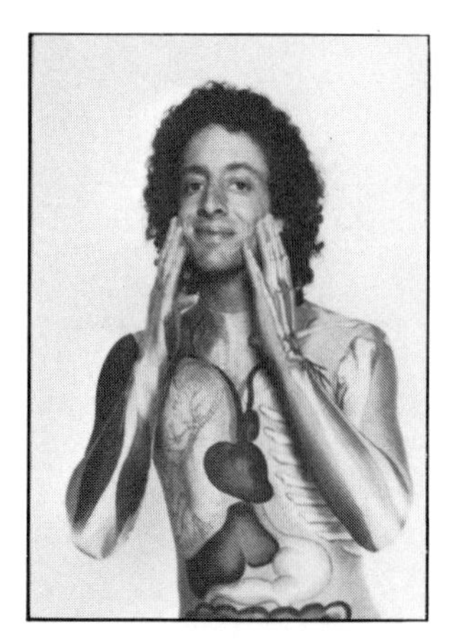

GLORIOUS SIGHT

Your eyes provide your brain with pictures of the outside world. If you want to become a better "photographer," here are some exercises you can do to improve your vision. Some of them were taught to me by an Eskimo hunter who has to rely on the sharpness of his sight to guide him home through the blinding-white Alaskan winter.

1. Sit comfortably on a chair or on the floor and imagine there is a giant clock in front of you. A clock so big it fills your entire field of vision. Keeping your head straight and still, use your eyes to look up at the number 12. Now look at the number 1, then 2, then 3, and slowly go around the

numbers of the clock until you get back to 12. Go two or three times around in the same direction and then rest. Close your eyes and relax for a minute. Now open your eyes and, starting again at the number 12, this time go backwards to 11, 10, 9, and so on, moving slowly and smoothly around until you are back at 12. Go two or three times around in this direction, then close your eyes for a while and relax.

2. Place this book upright on a table where you can easily see it and jump up and down while reading the next sentence.

I AM LEARNING HOW TO KEEP MY VISION STEADY WHEN I AM MOVING AROUND A LOT.

3. Stand or sit in a comfortable way and hold this book so the middle of the circle is lined up with the middle of your nose. If you have some music with a good strong beat, put it on. If not, set your own steady rhythm.

First look at the number 1. On the next beat, move your eye to the number 2. Next beat, to 3, and so on. At first your eyes will jump in search of the next number, but when you have done this exercise a few times, you'll be able to move your eyes in a smooth and steady fashion.

All of these exercises will sharpen your vision and develop eye-muscle control. Together, they'll increase your power of sight.

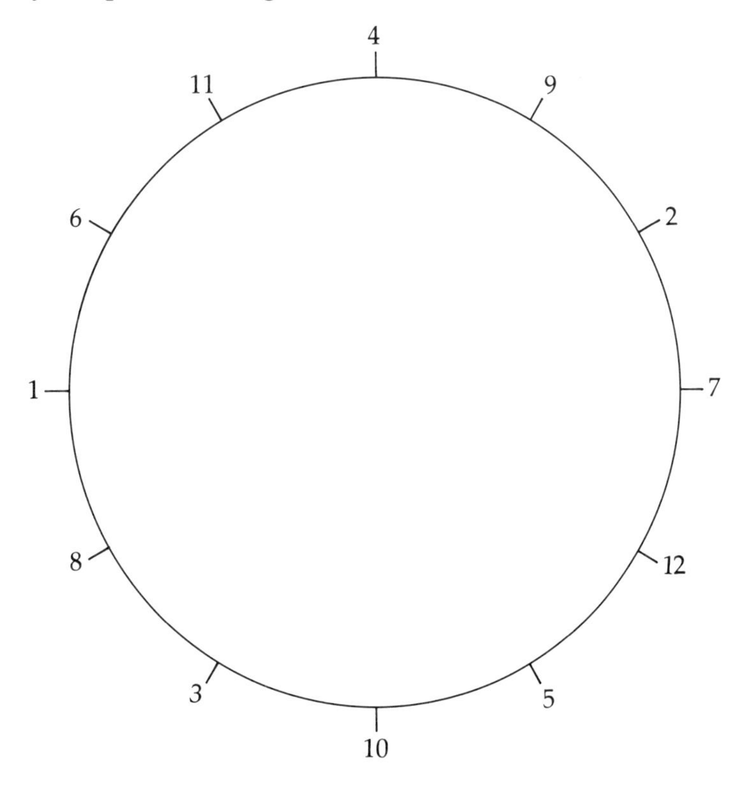

IN TOUCH

Blind people have a sense of touch that is far better than those of us who are sighted. The reason is that they depend upon it and use it much more often than we do. But touch is a sense that can be developed easily if you put in some time and effort.

Here are some exercises to help you:

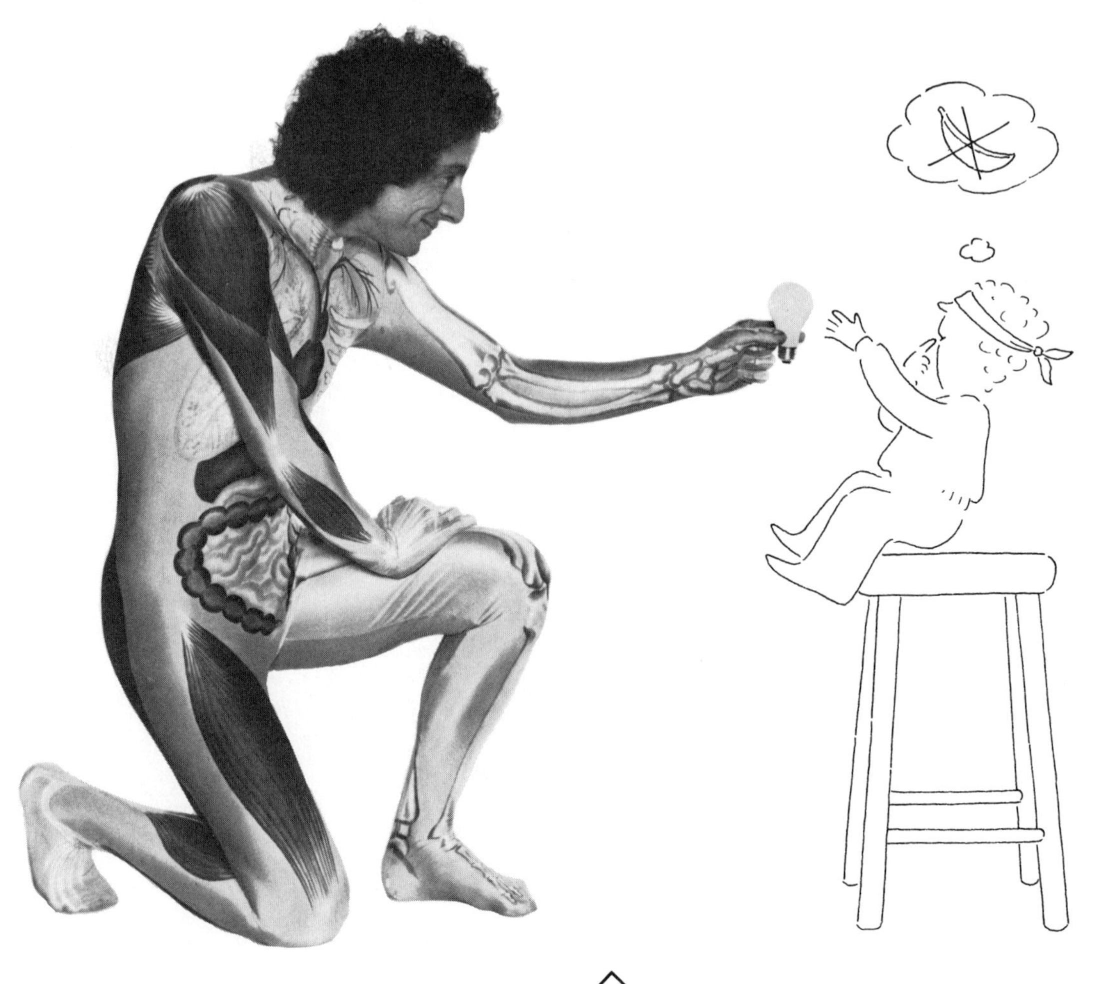

1. Sometime when you are in a familiar room, close your eyes (or have somebody put a blindfold on you) and walk around slowly. Let your hands do the "looking." Touch and feel things as you walk along. Try to guess what each object is just from the feel of it.

Do the same thing in a room that you don't know quite so well.

2. Put ten coins in your pocket. Two each of pennies, nickels, dimes, quarters, and half-dollars. Take your hand out of your pocket and jump around for a moment to make sure the coins get all mixed up. Now reach back into your pocket, pick up one of the coins between your fingers, and guess which one it is. Then take it out and check to see if you were right. If you were, put the coin down on a table. If you were wrong, drop it back into your pocket. Continue this exercise until your pocket is empty.

3. Practice slipping a key into a keyhole in the dark. At first you'll probably find it quite difficult, but soon your fingers will be able to guide the key in quickly and smoothly.

LOUD AND CLEAR

Many anthropologists (scientists who study the origins of the human race) believe that cave men and women had much better hearing than we do today. That's because they had to depend upon it to stay alive. If an animal was creeping through the underbrush, they had to be able to hear it in enough time to escape!

As the world became safer, people stopped relying on their sense of hearing to protect them from danger. One of the few times we use it now for this purpose is when we start to cross the street and jump back at the sound of a car horn.

Gradually we've lost some of the power that we once had. The following exercises, taught to me by the conductor of a symphony orchestra, will help you regain some of your natural hearing ability.

1. Collect four different coins—a penny, a nickel, a dime, and a quarter. Drop each coin, one at a time, on a table or desk top and listen carefully to the sound each one makes.

Now close your eyes and ask someone else to drop the coins for you while you guess which one it is. You can actually train your ears to hear the difference. You just have to concentrate and listen carefully.

2. Close your eyes and listen to the sounds all around you. See how many different ones you can hear. Try to figure out exactly what is making each sound.

3. Sometimes you have to be able to ignore sound so that you can concentrate on what you're doing. So right now, sit quietly and try to listen to just one sound. No matter what other noise there is, just keep concentrating on that one sound. Try to hear only that.

4. Next time you aren't quite sure which direction a sound is coming from, turning your head slowly from side to side will help you figure it out. Here's why:

When sound waves travel through the air, they reach one of your ears a fraction of a second before they reach the other. This difference in timing helps your brain calculate exactly where the sound is coming from. But sometimes the difference is so slight that it takes a little added effort to help locate the source of the sound. By moving your head slowly you are supplying your brain with extra information. Army scouts rely on this method to aid them in hearing the enemy approach.

You can sharpen your direction-finding ability by standing in a hall, closing your eyes, and figuring out which direction footsteps are coming from. Or from which end of the tunnel the subway will be arriving.

BALANCING ACT

When you were a baby, it took you months and months to learn how to stand up. There were two reasons for this:

1. You needed time to develop muscle strength.
2. You needed time to learn how to balance on two feet.

Without being able to balance, you'd spend your whole life just lying on the floor. No sitting, standing, walking, running, bike-riding, or skateboarding. That's because there is a very powerful force that pulls everything down to the Earth. It's called gravity. Your muscles aren't strong enough to fight against this force for long. You need to learn how to work *with* it! Working with gravity is called BALANCING!

The ancient Greeks knew how important it was to develop a fine sense of balance. They depended upon it in a very important area of their lives—athletics. Here are some of the exercises they designed for their children to practice.

1. Balancing objects. Greek children used coins, sticks, pottery, spearheads, etc., for this exercise. Nowadays you can work with the objects listed below:

   A coin
   A book on its end
   A pencil on your finger
   A broomhandle on your palm
   A jar lid
   A foot ruler

2. Balancing yourself. Practice balancing on:

   One foot for 30 seconds. Then the other foot.
   On one foot for 20 seconds with your eyes closed. Then the other foot.
   On tiptoes with your legs wide apart, for 30 seconds.
   On tiptoes with your legs close together, for 30 seconds.
   On one foot, on blocks that raise you 6 inches into the air, for one minute. Then on the other foot.
   On one arm and one leg, for one minute.
   On your head for 30 seconds.

3. Tape a one-inch-wide line on the floor with masking tape, or draw a line on the sidewalk with chalk. Make it about 10 feet long. Now walk, heel to toe, along the length. Then do it backwards.

4. Stand tall:

Bend your right knee, lift it and grasp it with both hands. Your left leg is not stiff, just straight. Bend over farther and touch your forehead to your knee. Straighten up, release your knee, and lower your leg.

Try it again on the other side.

INNER SENSE OF TIME

Adolf Baumeister, the famous clockmaker of Bremen, Germany, never wore a watch or had a clock in his own home, and yet he was never late for an appointment. As a matter of fact, he could always tell you within two or three minutes exactly what time it was. How did he do this? Through the following training method, which you can also use:

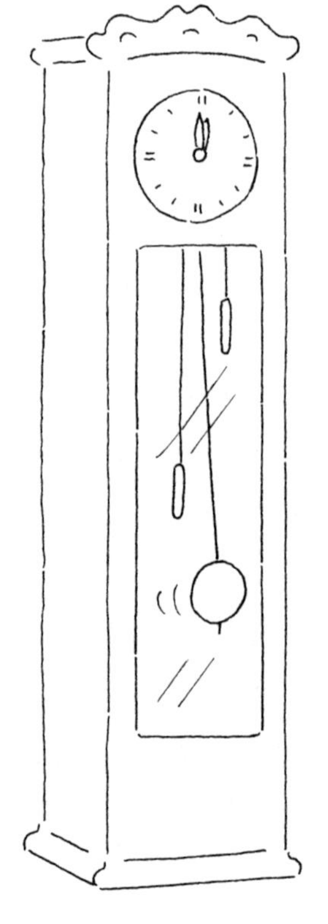

Step 1

Sit down comfortably in a chair, in front of a clock with a second hand. Now, close your eyes and open them when you think exactly five seconds have passed. Then check with the clock.

Did you do it? If you're like most people, you probably opened your eyes too soon. Try again. Do it over and over again until you can judge correctly on every try. Be sure not to count silently. The point is to "sense" the passage of time.

Step 2

Using the same method as before, close your eyes for 10 seconds. Then 15. Finally, 30.

Step 3

For this look at the clock to see the time. Now go out of the room and read a book or play a game—something that will take your mind off the time. When you "feel" inside that 15 minutes have passed, go back in and check the clock. Practice this step until you can accurately judge 15, 20, and 30 minutes.

Remember, the idea is to develop your *inner* sense of time passing, without actually thinking about it. You can practice this exercise whenever you want to by checking the time before you start an activity and again when you've finished, on each occasion trying to judge how much time has passed.

Step 4

Before going to bed at night, tell yourself that you'll wake up at a certain time the next morning. Let's say 8 A.M. Close your eyes and picture the number on an imaginary clock in your mind's eye. Then go to sleep and trust you will wake up at 8 A.M. sharp. Practice this exercise for several nights and you'll be amazed at how well you do.

THE FORCE OF THE MIND

In school you are taught math, English, science, history, and other subjects, all of them designed to educate your mind. But the world is filled with things to learn and ideas to think about. School can't teach you everything.

There are some things that you have to learn yourself. This chapter will help you develop some of very special forces of the Mind.

REMEMBERING

Everything you've ever seen, heard, thought, felt, learned, or experienced is stored away in your memory. But for some reason there are many times when you'll have trouble remembering something you know. Why? Well, scientists still don't know the answer. There are certain exercises, however, that will help strengthen the power of your memory.

1. Take a deck of cards and place it facedown on a table. Pick up one card and look at it just for five seconds. Put it down. Can you remember which card it was? Now pick up two cards. Put them down. What were they?

Try it again with three cards, holding them up only as long as you held up the first card. Can you remember all three?

It helps to close your eyes for a moment and picture them in your hand as they were. Keep practicing until you can remember as many as ten cards.

2. There are really two kinds of memory, Picture Memory and Word Memory. Putting them together helps build up your power to remember. This exercise is called Eyewitness.

The next time you meet someone, look at what he or she is wearing and describe it to yourself in words. Don't say it out loud, say it mentally: "That kid is wearing a red belt, red pants, a blue shirt, . . ." The more details, the better you'll remember.

3. Before you go to bed at night, review your day. Starting with the morning when you got up, remember what you ate, what you did, whom you saw, etc.

At first, don't worry about remembering the whole day. Just try to recall what happened in the morning. As the week passes, add on hours until you can remember the whole day in detail. You'll find that your memory for all things has become a lot sharper.

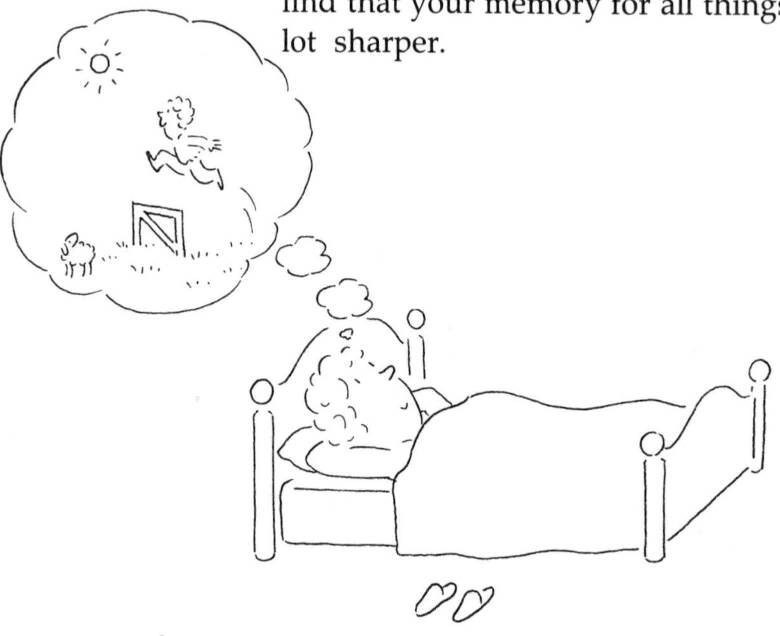

CONCENTRATED FORCE

Concentration means the ability to direct your thoughts and fix your attention on one particular thing. This may sound easy, but true concentration takes quite a lot of effort.

Have you ever seen a magnifying glass focusing the rays of the sun? The energy gets so concentrated that it can burn a hole right through whatever it is the rays are falling on. In a similar way, when you concentrate all of your thoughts on something, let's say a question or a problem, you'll be able to burn a mental hole right through it and glimpse the answer on the other side.

Here are some exercises to help you develop the power of concentration.

1. Look at a watch or a clock with a second hand. Focus on the movement of that hand as it sweeps around the dial. Watch it make one complete revolution and do not let your eyes or mind wander. When you are honestly sure that you have kept your concentration focused for a full minute, you will be well on the way to developing Concentrated Force.

2. Focusing on movement of the second hand as before, count from one to ten and back again mentally. Do this very slowly so it takes a full minute to count all the numbers. Practice this so you can do it three times in a row.

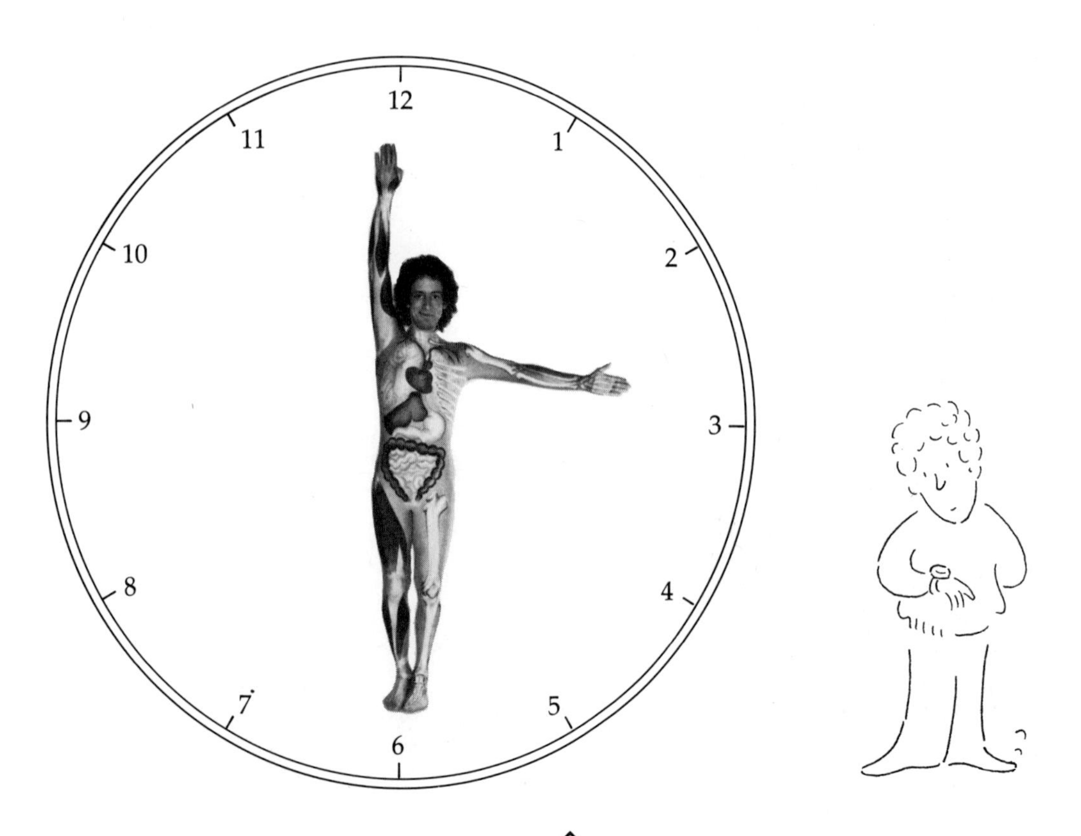

3. While you have your eyes closed, think about the room you are in. Concentrate on seeing a picture of the room in your mind's eye. Then open your eyes and look around the room again. Did it look this way when you had your eyes closed? Look carefully and concentrate on the furniture and the objects on the tables, shelves, and walls. Now get a piece of paper and pencil and go into another room and write down as many of the things that were in the room as you can remember. When thinking about the room, concentrate on making a picture of it mentally to help you remember how it looked.

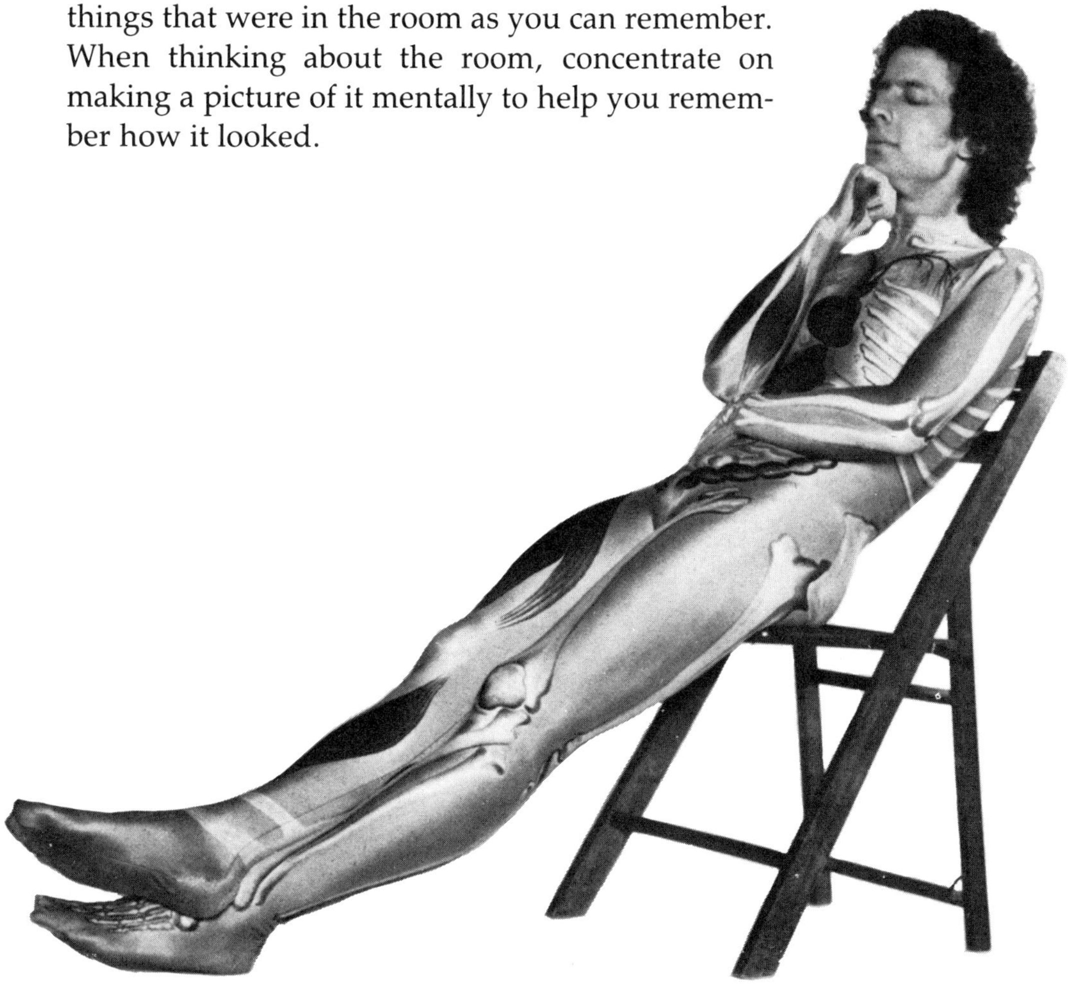

THE FORCE OF COMMUNICATION

We are all members of the human family. Communicating with each other clearly and creatively brings joy and love into our lives and brings us closer together.

Let's develop some new communication skills. . . .

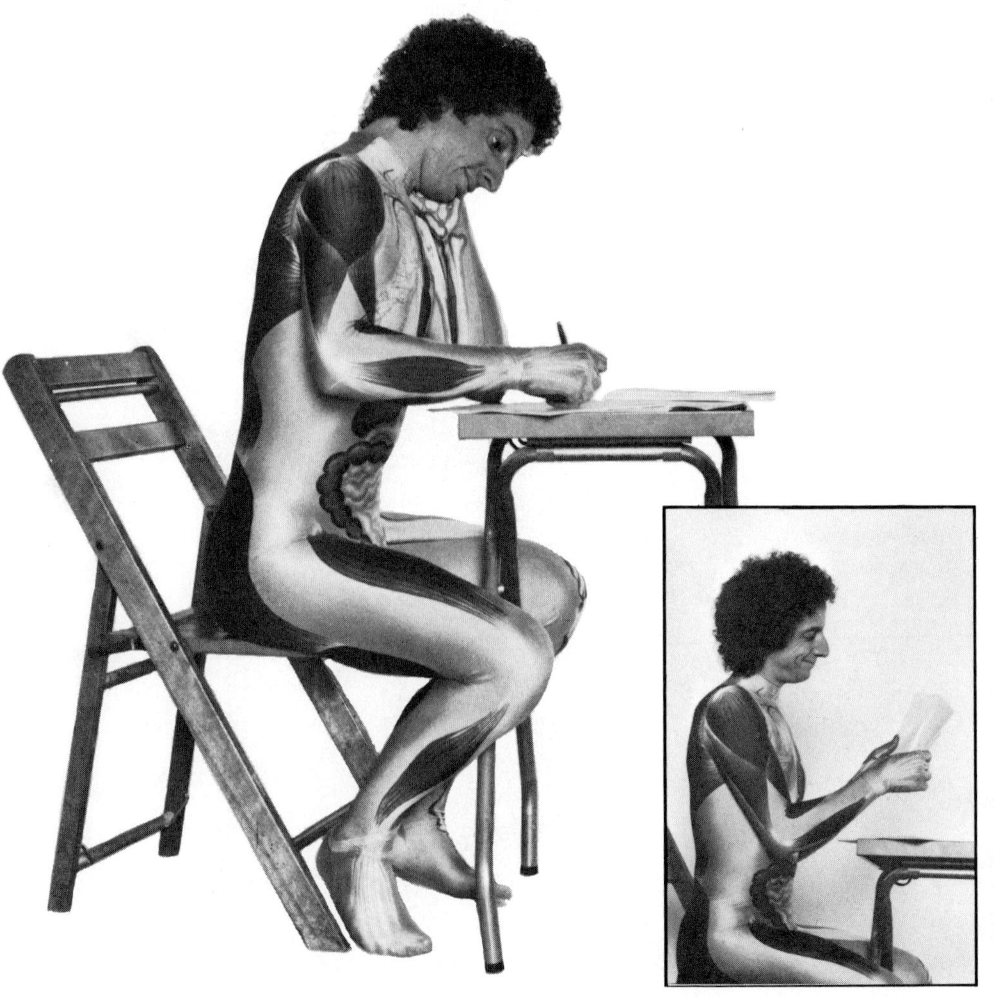

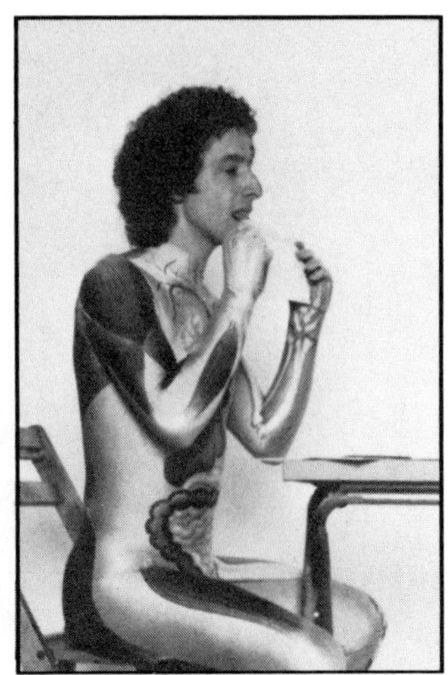

WRITE-ON

Writing is one of the most important ways we have of communicating. It gives us the ability to pass on thoughts and feelings to people living in other places or in the future. You can even communicate with yourself by jotting down notes throughout the day about things that interest you and reading them later on.

The skill of penmanship is taught to us in school, yet once we've learned it, we hardly ever practice it again. Here is a group of exercises that you can do to have some fun with writing, while you increase your manual skill.

1. Write your name with your eyes closed. Try to do it on a straight line.

2. While you are writing your name (this time with your eyes open) move one of your feet around in a circle. You'll find that writing becomes much harder. If your name comes out pretty clear, then your foot has probably been following the pattern of your hand and not moving in circles. Try again.

With enough practice, you'll be able to do both things at the same time.

3. Try mirror writing. Place a mirror on a piece of paper, and, looking into it, write this sentence:

THINGS LOOK STRANGE WHEN I WRITE LIKE THIS.

4. Write the alphabet backwards.

5. Take a familiar poem and write it backwards, the last word first. See how fast you can go.

THINGS LOOK STRANGE WHEN I WRITE LIKE THIS.

READ ON

Reading is great exercise for your mind and your eyes. A brilliant editor developed these exercises to increase your Reading Force.

1. Read the following sentences correctly. All the words have been spelled backwards.

gnidaeR si taerg esicrexe rof ruoy dnim dna ruoy seye. tuB ti erus si egnarts ot ees ti sdrawkcab.

2. Read the following unspaced sentences.

Ifbookswerewrittenlikethisthentheywouldbeawholelotshorter. Youcouldsavealotofspacebutldon'tthinkthatitwouldbeworthit. Itwouldtakepeoplehoursjusttoreadsomesimplesentences.

3. Read the following unspaced sentences. Every other word is backwards.

NowsihtisehtstrangestdnikofgnidaerIknihtIevaheverenod. I'mdalg theyt'nodteachtithisyawinloohcs.

4. Now try this one.

It really takes talent to be able to read
words when they're printed upside down like this.
I'm enjoying figuring them out.

SPEECH! SPEECH!

One of the most wonderful gifts human beings have is the power of speech. We begin learning how to talk by listening to our parents, family, and friends. By the time we go to school we're communicating pretty well. If people understand us, we don't bother trying to improve this ability.

There is a story about an ancient Greek orator named Demosthenes. He wanted to make speeches, but he stuttered and stumbled over his words so much that nobody could understand him. Yet he was determined to speak more clearly. He used to practice his speeches with his mouth full of marble-sized pebbles until his words became clearer and clearer.

For most people this is not a safe or practical thing to do, but here are some vocal exercises you can try. To speak clearly, you must use different parts of your mouth.

1. To loosen up your tongue say the following words quickly and smoothly:

   land, lad, last, lame, lean
   lawn, ledge, let, left, limb
   letter, long, light, like, look
   loot, little, loss, live, love

A really good one-word exercise for your tongue is to say "lilly" twenty-five times in a row.

2. To warm up your lips say the following:

paper, party, people, pet, pig
picture, place, pony, pull, put
pack, pad, palm, peak, pin
pole, puff, pine, pot, pool

A really good one-word exercise for your lips is to say "bebe" twenty-five times in a row.

3. Here are words to warm up your jaw muscles. Your teeth have to become involved:

zeal, zebra, zero, zest, zinc
zoo, zone, zen, zany, zip
zig, zag, zoom, zounds, zoology
zippy, zodiac, zoid, zonal, zooks

A really good one-word exercise using your teeth is "zaza" said twenty-five times in a row.

4. For your lips and tongue together say:

plump, plow, play, plot, please
plan, plane, plight, pledge, plead
blimp, blame, black, blunt, blue
blow, blood, bleed, blind, block

5. For your teeth and lips together say:

face, fast, fact, fame, fake
file, fuss, feel, fine, fee
fade, fail, film, five, faint
faith, feed, food, fear, finish

SIGN LANGUAGE

There are some people who are unable to speak and hear. They are completely deaf. But there is a way that they *can* communicate with each other and with people who hear. It's called sign language. If you want to increase your power of communication and learn to share ideas and feelings with the deaf, practice "speaking" with your hands, using Sign Language. Here's the alphabet:

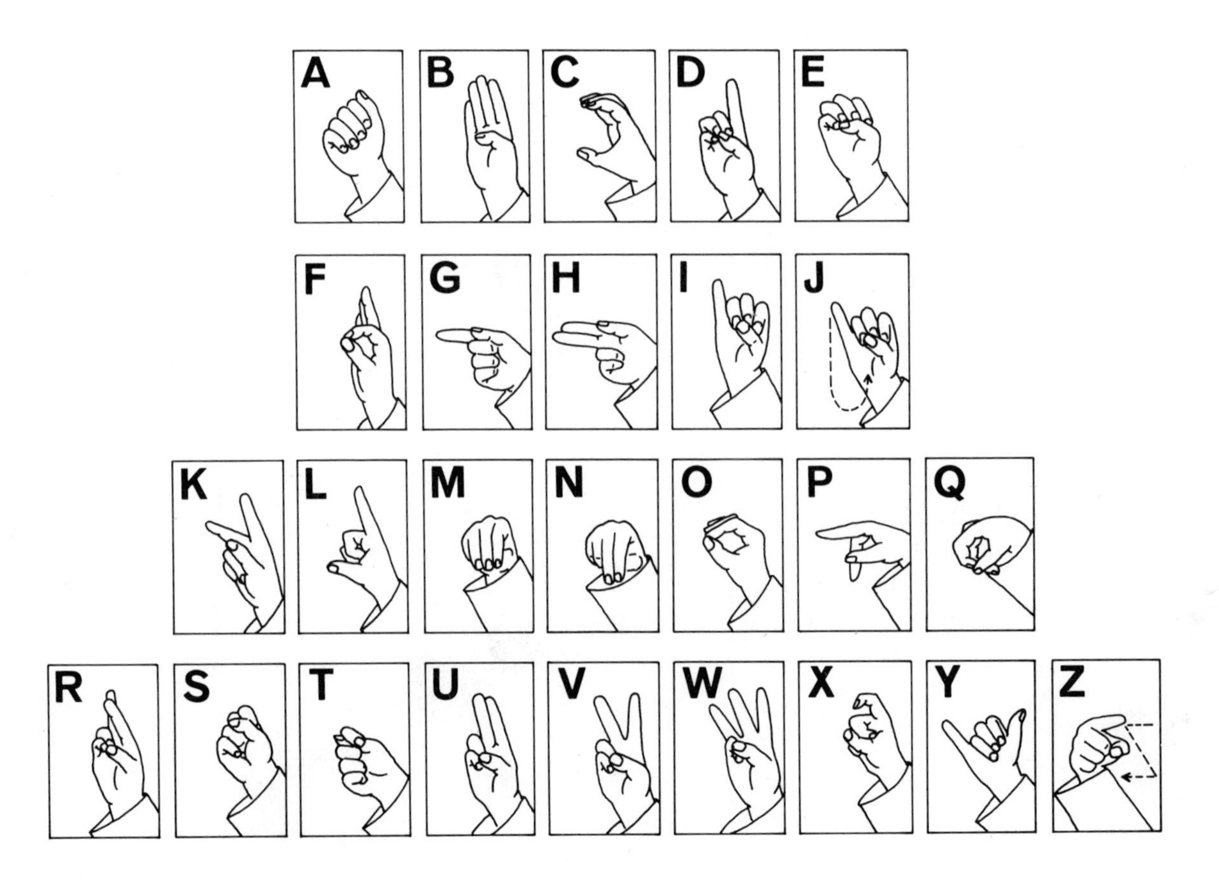

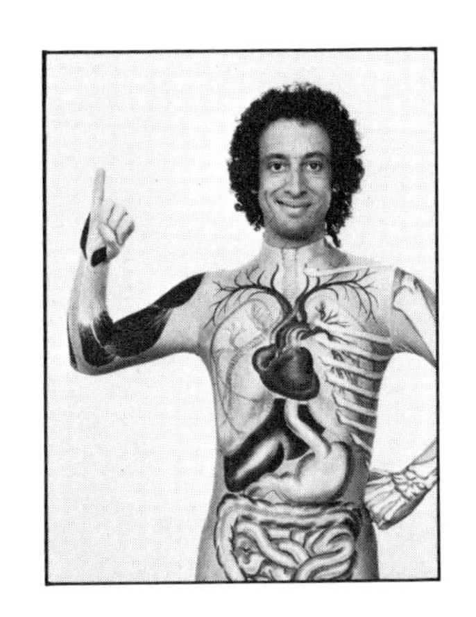

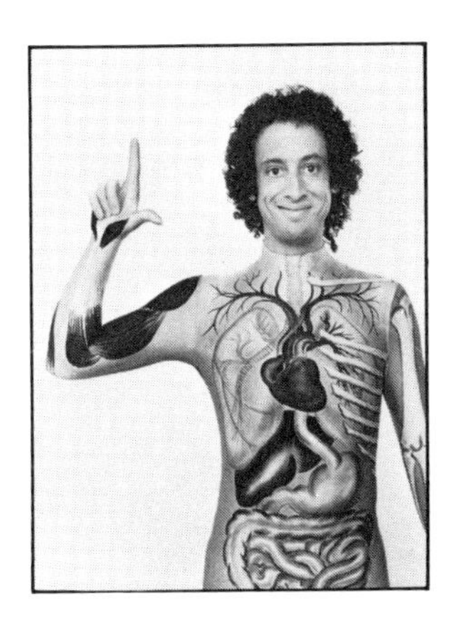

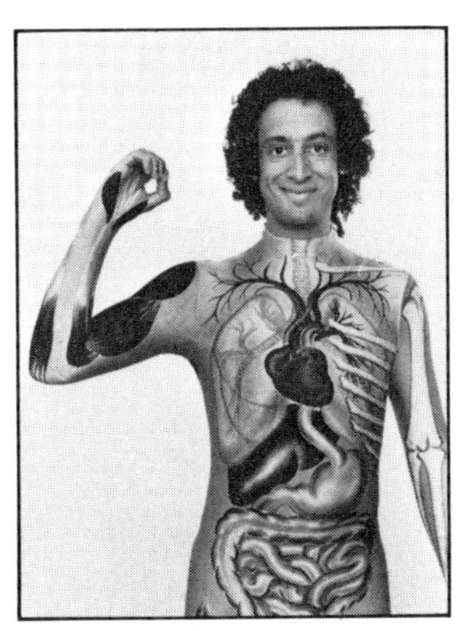

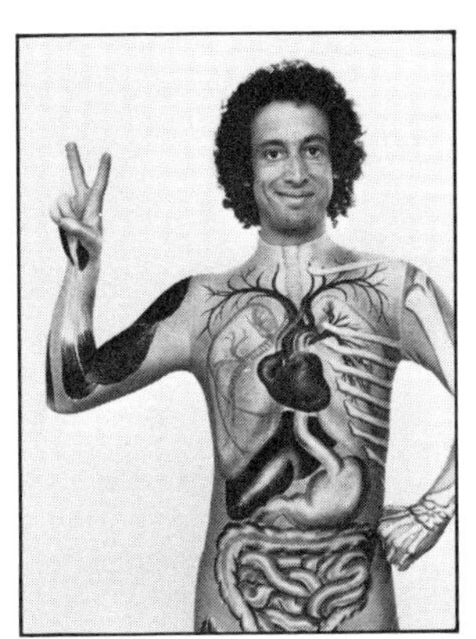

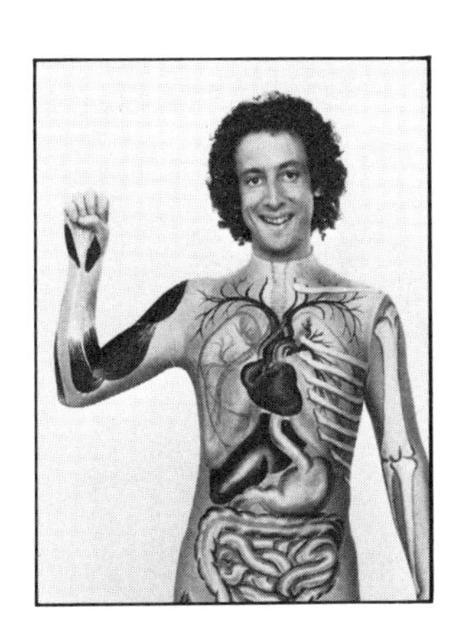

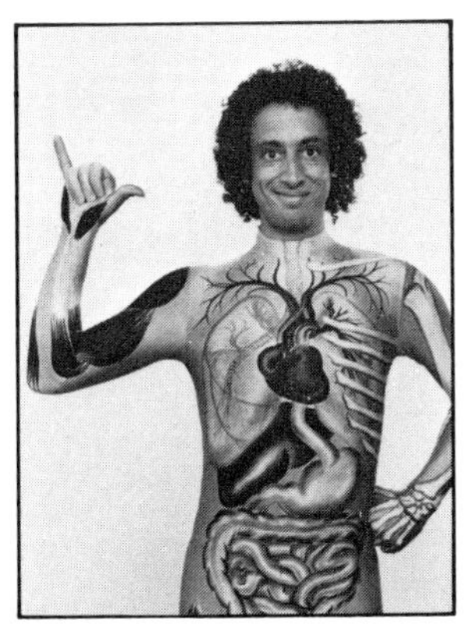

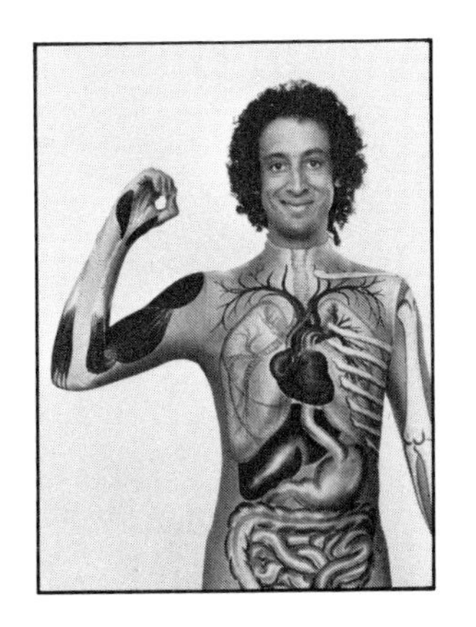

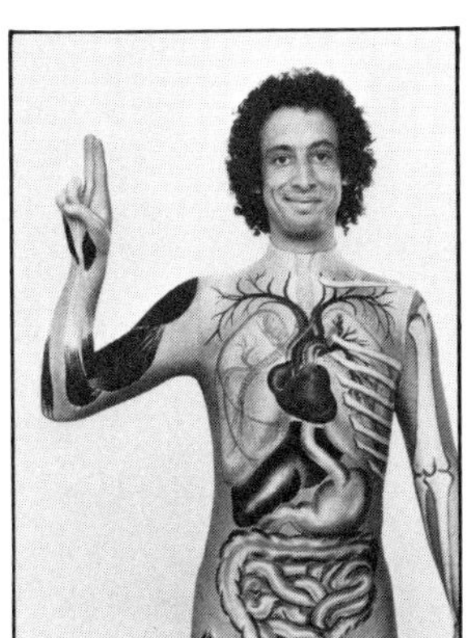

FINAL RECIPE

When all is said and done, *you* are the only one who can develop the Force Inside You. All the exercises in my book can help point the way, but it's up to you to follow through. Just reading isn't enough, you've got to practice them over and over to increase your force.

If you want, you can think of them as Recipes. I've listed the ingredients and now it's up to you to mix them together and add the most important part—your active participation.

As you develop the Force Inside You, you'll probably discover all kinds of new exercises you can do. That's just great! There is no limit to the things you can do.

Finally, I want to wish you the best of luck and I hope you'll enjoy yourself as you grow and expand the Force Inside You.

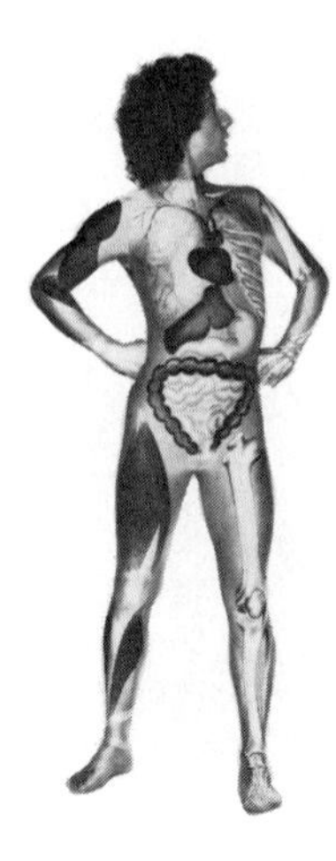

INDEX

Message on page 59
I love you